AUP New Poets 4

AUP New Poets 4

chris
TSE

erin
SCUDDER

harry
JONES

AUCKLAND UNIVERSITY PRESS

Some of the poems in this book have appeared in the following publications:
Sport (Harry Jones) and *Turbine* and *Cha* (Chris Tse).

First published 2011

Auckland University Press
University of Auckland
Private Bag 92019
Auckland 1142
New Zealand

ISBN 978 1 86940 474 1

Publication is kindly assisted by

National Library of New Zealand Cataloguing-in-Publication Data
Jones, Harry, 1952-
AUP new poets. 4 / Harry Jones, Erin Scudder, Chris Tse.
ISBN 978-1-86940-474-1
1. New Zealand poetry—21st century. I. Scudder, Erin.
Il. Tse, Chris, 1982-. Ill. Title.
NZ821.3—dc 22

Author photographs by Leighton Tse (Chris Tse); Chris Parker (Harry Jones);
and Emma London (Erin Scudder)

Cover design by Christine Hansen
Printed by Printlink, Wellington

Contents

Harry Jones : Beyond Hinuera

chris
TSE

Sing Joe

Dig

after Seamus Heaney

Our first back yard hugged
the prickled slopes
of Kelson.

I watched my father dig and
tear his way   through bush and clay
to find that richer soil.

The spicy scent of gorse, the path
        he zigzagged.

And beyond him, decades
        and oceans away,
his father stooping to dig
gathering ginger and spring onion;
        dreams of richer days.

  •

Between my finger and my thumb
the sticks rest.

  •

Below the surface lies
a history of chopsticks.
                In the days
of new sight we clung to comfort
as a sign of success.

Eight treasure soups,
the finest teas
        ivory and bone over
        wood and plastic.

  •

I'll dig
        with them.

Chinese whispers

Fog on our minds.

Whispers   in the creak

of photo album spines.

Tear open the years

discover what history holds court

in the red   of our blood.

Cross-fade

He cradles his son and wife, makes promises
out of paper – promises that will wait
in darkened rooms.
                                In time
they will be torn and cursed in despair.

Rooms will grow
                        darker.

And like water, secrets will find their way
into everything
muddy the heart   and drown all hope.

            .

She begged him to stay, asked neighbours
to help change his mind. She did not want
to be one of those wives   left to wait

in a maddening shroud, with false glimmers
of return or reunification   a doll married
to dust   on the highest shelf.

She knew she might never follow.

            .

Held in his exhibition of final moments:

her smile like pinched steel
eyes armed with trust.

This is for the best.
[speaker unknown]

            .

The seas   hold him tight
and he puts the luck of his loved ones
back into the hidden

where unforgettable voices
outstay their welcome
like a child with just one song.

Water and new light pass in circles
terrors in the night seize his tongue.
Her last expression weathers his resolve.

He will ask for forgiveness a thousand times over
but the silence that follows
is the crow he can't shake off.

                    .

Held in her exhibition of the passing months:

an edgeless community cradling
gossip in tea-cups

letters arrive with no invitation
for response.

Landing (A Thursday, A Calm)

Call on those perfect gods and light will turn.

He left familiar doors and their Protector

for a sharper grace   to seek what the stars sing.   *The shore is here!*

                    Water loose in the air   breath caught in the stillicide

unbearable itch in his mouth   white noise crashing through all thoughts.

          There is no design.   When it comes to solutions he dances in circles

though some would say   (through gritted teeth)   it was never his turn to lead.

                    A stained line   on his prosperous map

his wife's belief in unison   a wave in the dark

               with nowhere to crash.

The *Maheno* deposits its contribution   to the growing land

          of plenty.   In single file he passes through

tax paid, no photo provided   fingerprints taken for identification.

     Joe Choy Kum   *arr: 23 October 1919*   *#853*

Sing Joe (1)

All new things   pass through like fire
                        their trail: cinders and maps
that sing and spark.

        The word for *untouched soil*
is now yesterday's ode   long forgotten
                        by the time letters reach China

        with his new name.

        •

So what's in a name change anyway, Mr Joe?
A mere reversal of two little words.

Oh how loose and elastic
                        their ink realigns

the names of these new arrivals
            like tiny hearts plucked from quivering branches

of their grand trees
unceremoniously recast in English.

Now that the eyes scroll across
            Western pages   *Kum* takes charge

while *Joe* fills quiet minutes
                        reduced to secret coda.

And even with a full, heavy heart the lives of your two names
            could never be married

the parallel of drifting boats in fractured light
the unsaid   the unbreakable   guiding your blind hand.

        •

Sing Joe when the fever is high and your eyes turn
        to China and all that you left:
                a holding space.

Sing Kum when you knew   this was no life
        to live in
constant state of emergency

        all these Joe Chinamans   side by side
                with the same
dreams and the same face

        a name for every occasion, season and country
                born from footprints you never thought
        twice about casting

like the man at sea
        with his head lost
                in the colour of caution.

Stability

You'll never be soft enough, strong enough, white enough, bold enough, clean like the air, faithful like God's sheep, quiet enough, loud enough, horses broken to weather the fall, the right safety, the right machine, bright enough, plenty enough, earth enough, on the axis of the motherland, cruel enough, hard enough to last the winter months, to keep the tide see-sawing, dry enough, too far gone enough, mirror enough, sweet enough, crushed enough by an anchor heart, enough to fill each room with her absent shape, life goes on with enough busy keys and secret doors to keep the veil dressed, houses straight not akimbo, enough tea for a meal held together by salt, hinged on gratitude, no tongue satisfied, starvation as treason, as husband, wife, mother, father, early enough, late enough, pure enough.

The Second Wife

Splintered roots,
new roots and
shadows cast on past lives.

But shadows don't erase
they just conceal and feed
the knot at the back of his head.

Strings across land and sea
tied to the feet of his first wife,
the new bride poised with scissors.

Grieving mechanism

In a single night
      she breaks
three bowls and wakes the neighbours twice.

Words are exchanged
      the next morning.
She's taken to roaming the village

swallowing painful prayers
until her voice
      dries up.

The only message
for her husband:
      I am a fool to have believed you.

The children know
      to avoid her.
She may as well be a widow,

carry a dead dog
on her back
      and seal her fate.

Setting son

A son follows
       his wandering father,
leaves behind two sleeping brothers

and a lonely mother, whose heart fell
for this event
          many years ago.

What is the heart but a pulp of stories?
       Hers already filled
with the news

he will send of his journey –
new school,
        step-mother,

half-brother, all the things
she doesn't want
         to hear.

He will find a place to run
         a loopy
      song to sing, under

vast southern skies.
      Let English form
         at the corners of

        his mouth, let him taste
open spaces
       with his bare feet.

These days

She sits at the edge
of front door and
outside world, her hand resting
on the only photograph
she has of her husband
his name still static
in her throat.

The girl betrothed to her son
is cleaning inside.
She shifts and creaks
through each tombstone room,
stacking dishes in the kitchen,
polishing the table
with determination.

Very soon her son will return
to take his bride
back to New Zealand.
But what of his mother –
will he leave her
to fill this house with sound
alone?

The sun hooks her eye
and in the light
she recollects days of
tender architecture,
when all she hoped for
was a life of family
to spill out at her grateful feet.

Sing Joe (2)

Never underestimate   the potential energy

nested in three noble syllables   read from right to left.

Father and son with different appendages: *Kum, Wing.*

You seemed unfazed to start anew   an abandonment of past graces

while your son reset   from *Joe* to *Wing* and back again

with bank accounts in each name   like conjoined rooms to store each breath.

    .

This is where our table of contents splinters

and the hue of countless generations suddenly shifts.

As the younger entries begin to spread their ink

our once-unifying name arches further from the clan

cuts itself a groove   in the family's bristled opera.

We carry its melody on everyday breaths   but can't undo the words.

Plans

The First Wife takes a look around the house –
the garden needs a fruit tree for sweetness.

.

A letter arrives from her son
with arrangements for her trip to New Zealand.

Finally, she will meet her grand-daughters –
there could be no greater gift.

.

But there is one condition: she cannot be the wife
of a married man.

When she arrives she must be
a different woman, an *aunty*.

.

She takes one last look around the house
and imagines the fruit trees in her husband's garden.

Waking the ghost

Over the decades, the only thing
worth archiving has been
her halo's glare – but now
he has never felt
            so regretful
for leaving her behind with
nothing but sky to protect her.
He soldiered through
            bold and confused
and summoned the huge tide
to sink everything
when the pain crept in.
What remains is just
a little time
to fill otherwise empty days.
He sits at windows undressing
the street before him and
on rare occasions
            when he can bring
himself to acknowledge it
                        he sees her
in the strangest things –
a child's clumsy wave,
a spiralling bird
            – but he must
tell himself that this is just
her ghost finally woken and
soon she will be here
to meet her grand-daughters
and face
            his new family.
The pale sky steps down.
There is no sound
when it turns from its duties.

True stories

No grand welcome, no arms thrown

    around this old woman's neck.

Heads face forward and we are told

    to behave – she is an aunty

and that's that. But eventually we will

    piece her together, we will discover

how her blood flows into ours.

    We will whisper *grandmother*

to ourselves and nod in agreement

    at our cleverness. Of course

the questions are endless, like the snakes

    that infest her bedtime stories

entrenched in our sheets – itchy slither,

    too fast to hold this loaded truth.

Husband to Wife

With the road tied
into your hair

and your tongue
bent to speak only
          true words
you will find your way back to Guangzhou.

It's a haze there in the room
where you keep my photo,

windows boarded up
the outside world erased,
a thousand hearts beat
out of time in your mouth.

O sweet one – what has become
          of you?

Now you are
no wilder
nor more dangerous
than that stifled song in your throat.

Come, I want to treat you
rice wine and dim sums.

Turn the page

They say to me: I knew your mother's   father's   father.
Every day he took pause
with gentle eyes
          to survey his domain
his privilege
his untangled tongue.
                    The resetting of names
moments of peace   lost in his own landslide.

        .

I say: no more weather stories   please.
No more falling in love with the ghosts of ideas.
Give me the marching band
                    all the way from hello
          to ashes   to ashes.

The inconvenient coat rack

stands guard
by the front door
punctuates all entry and exit.

But anyone walking by
could fell this tree
with the slightest brush

even I, a small boy,
could upset its balance
        bring down its wet-weather
baggage for us to wear.

Sometimes I hide
under its foliage   in the heat
and darkness of the inner layer

stew in the smell
        of mothballs   and wait
for unsuspecting adults.

All of Ma Ma's clothes
smell like mothballs.
We have dubbed it

        the smell of Hong Kong
because everything from there
emits that arid perfume.

Even the money that is sent over
        in lucky red envelopes.

Even the money is spiced
with mothballs.

Uncle Willie

Afternoon tea
at the Oriental Fruit Company, Petone,
requires a wedge of pineapple cheese
and Uncle Willie is always the first
to dash down Jackson Street to procure it.
Any excuse to get out of the shop.

Meals are different if one works
in a fruit shop; our fingers
know stories of rotten carrots and cabbages.
Only the freshest for Willie –
he'll make a fuss if served leftovers.
The key to keeping him happy is to top
everything off with a shiny fried egg; you'd think
he was just given a solid gold nugget.

While he's distracted,
lovingly tending to his egg,
we'll sneak upstairs
and hunt for the black shoe polish he insists
is what keeps his hair so mysteriously dark.
Women make you grey, we heard
an adult say once, which could explain
bachelor Willie's grey-free calm.

The only scandals we ever find
are his lusty magazines, tucked behind
the elixirs in the bathroom cupboard.
We finger the pages painted with bikinis
and listen carefully for the give-away crack
of Willie on floorboards.

Baby Joe

If he had a name
we would not be allowed
            to say it –

a paperweight sound
collecting dust
in every corner of our hearts

with nowhere to go but fade
into our secret history
caged in silent outlaw.

We are not to speak
of him nor
the last nine months

dinner table taboo
emotion best kept
behind closed doors.

But we can
blame the traffic
the nurses   the pneumonia.

He has filled this house
with questions
that tug   like little pincers.

Where do missing sons
take their mothers' hearts?

Finding the body

That night we came home to a house
of black windows – a warm welcome

for burglars and omens – the first sign
of trouble, panic in the blood.

.

The phone was pushed into my hands,
an operator already asking for details

I couldn't bring myself to say, my origami
heart already unfolding itself for tragedy.

Mum screamed for us
not to come into the bedroom.

.

When the ambulance had been and gone,
we stole a look –

the black webby stain
where a head had landed

sang to us for nights and nights
danced chills through our little bones.

Drift on

She slept for weeks – lines mapping her face, every part of her so much smaller. I'd sit by her bed gripping her hands; those frail fingers once folded paper boats for us to race and taught us how to colour neatly within the lines. In the end she needed us to turn the shower tap on every night, a chore I would later grow to miss.

And then it happened. One day after maths school my brother ran to meet me outside our parents' shop: *Ma Ma has died.*

I was the last to know. Suddenly the moment was fighting for room in my head among the angles and denominators, and I didn't know where to put the news.

It was also the day I learned how to draw snakes. At the time I thought acquiring this skill had sealed all fates.

Everyone told me that it would all be OK now, but the red in Dad's eyes and the hushed wooden tones we had shrouded ourselves in said otherwise.

That night I set the broken English of a Chinese magazine to a tune I'd picked up at school. Dad caught me singing and snapped.

Rootseeking missions

Day 1 of 28: the air holds new arrangements. We inhale,
hard and dangerous   never certain of the land we breathe.

•

Foshan cityscape at night – the only bar we find
is Leopard Boy and its randy inhabitants.

Wallets primed for overpriced spirits,
inhibitions left at the door.

In the morning   I settle
for sandwiches on my budget.

•

Most of the time we brave the mysteries:
plan trips to markets, clubs to raid.

We visit tourist attractions, contemporary shopping,
12 forbidden sights – our own ancestral excursions.

•

An eventful morning   the afternoon a little low.
Stand up to the scale; descend the Great Wall with little fanfare.

•

A silk haze of comedown after a full day.
Buddhism is the perfect drink for a winter's night.

•

Tiananmen Square: a significant performance.
Beijing magic.   We are attractions.

•

After weeks of buses, smoky taxis and a nation of Asian drivers
we throw the road from our hotel then lose our way to the next
    essential bar.

We notice China returned in the middle of the night
stitched together   with a Mandarin slur

which equates to nothing more than a celebratory excursion
of drunken apologies to the locals.

.

A hutong house reminds me of old Chinese TV shows.
The rickshaw circuit is spiky; we race for compensation.

.

One Chinese bar too far:
I feel fine afterwards   if a little disgusted.

.

I will miss waking up to fresh slippers
and over-zealous breakfasts.

.

All we need is history. A group portrait is proof enough –
the glitz of their tradition essentially a variety show.

.

Mornings of constant surprise   safety aside.
We start bright.

The family village

We are no longer strangers

to the paths of the family name

or its uncanny signposts.

The Joe chin. The Joe appetite.

In the belly of the family house

we offer incense at the top of a ladder.

A series of photographs from New Zealand

stops at 1985.

Pale to think of the darkened space

our Gung Gung slept in,

an empty bed now left to wait

for gold to fill its frame.

Something holds us to this pivot

point   from which the world

extends to a bread-crumb trail.

Tonight the air will ring with peace

as the weight of expectation is finally lifted.

After sharing this past

our giddy hearts will keep us   on right paths.

Deracinate

In this terracotta haze   my skin reads
      like foxed pages   yesterday's news
forged by the trial and error of endangered life.
This country   built on a heart
of borders   between old and new
every life a soldier   caught up in uneasy grace.

      Just another chink
in my armour.   Just another son missing
in a long line of dislocations
from the motherland
      from a mother tongue
          that licks at the hollow
of my mouth   down
to each last beat
of my difficult language.

      This talk of *the other* that trails
my every move back home
speaks not of defiance, but of blood-clot guilt.
Here, like evidence on trial,
      it pushes me across
every defined border
only to end up on my own side   still
where the verdict
      is my scarlet letter.

      Of course it mattered back then too,
possibly even more so –
not knowing which crayons to use at school
    for family portraits,
      and if it wasn't my name
      or my lunchbox contents

it was the Chinese tongue
    I so easily surrendered

to the playground government
all my colours   running in the wash.

    These days it seems I'm losing
myself again   more than ever
reborn in China
    like every other disconnected branch
split straight down the middle
    and walked out into proof.
They can see who I really am
all soil and tears   the product of fearless journey
    and the settler dream
when all I want   is to be brave
in safety with my inherited demons.

    I am but a tourist   a counterfeit
in their nights of private games,
    scattered on the wind
    a million leaves to the score.
I bring nothing but
    a selfish search   and a claim to belong.

Behind the safety of hotel windows
    protected from the vice-like grip
    of beggar kids
where curtains divided
    reveal this country
for what it is:
grey   inconsistent
    and
for reasons unknown   utterly addictive.

erin
SCUDDER

Admission

The Former Pastor

He tells me about a cow
that went missing from his farm,
a cow that was pregnant by the time that he found it.
He tells me this as though
it is definitely of interest to me,
as though I know about the country, or anything about animals.
He always talks to me
as though we know each other,
and are accustomed to trading remarks across the dinner table,
or while leaning against a fence.
There's a longing in him that displaces formality.
He redefines the word *pastoral*, for me. His conversation forms the
    backdrop
for a sort of ease to which I did not know I was entitled.

Confession

Do you have an eye of God?
Can you sense the lack in me?

A man goes loping
by the shelves.

He has pastoral shoulders.
He has a beard that aches for talk.

But no –
I see what I want.

It's me who aches to talk
beside the sagging shelves.

I entertain the notion that somebody like him
could, with a loping motion,

forgive me for everything
I want to say.

Ancient March

I have spent a night in the hospital.
I have not spent a night.
I have had a night to remember –
I can't remember about my night.
I woke up and my boyfriend said
I don't want you to be scared and the doctor said
I said to the boyfriend I am scared, I am scared.
I remember from then on in scenes.
I am scared I said to the boy.

I, said the doctor, want to talk to you.
I am the one that he wants to talk to well how about that
    and how would I know.
I am the last person who would know.
I put my red feet on the floor well after all
I remember about my feet.
I had to go to the other room.
I listened: the physician said may
I have a word with you in the other room.
I had wounds like somebody else's.

I was still getting out of myself.
I was coming out of anaesthetic – well they did not tell me but
I was not still myself.
I'd like to know where I am before I have to talk to you,
I,
I could have said to the doctor.
I would like a word with you.
I would like you to tell me something about myself.

I'm a clam.
I'm a clam today.
I'm a clam on your beach.
I mean something to you but
I'm a shell to itself.

I know about the body, said the doctor. Well,
I said, then you tell me.
I don't think you know about history.

I'll stay here.
I'll otherwise go forward from here to where?
I, reading the moment again, am not convinced I shall, am not
    convinced
I did. I wanted something for my feet.
I wanted you not to peer at me with giant red terrified eyes,
    horrified.
I wanted comfort.
I, bewildered, I,
I lost a night and you were more scared than me.

Cranes

Inside the hospital lobby,
we pause beside the lifts.
On the directory, the clinic is listed –
that's a surprise.
This ride
up to heaven –
I would be beside
myself without you, here.

The wind rattles round,
but the cranes don't sway.
The old façade – the one they're tearing down – reminded me
of Gatsby, all globe-top lamp-posts and
creamy steps. Our steps
move to the left –
then to the side. Our arms
fly open and snap shut like fans.

I was looking for the future,
and saw some cranes over the harbour.
They always move slowly –
myopic, lumbering.
I go to sleep picturing the cranes.
They hold a vigil over the town,
poised to bow down,
ready to lift up something very heavy,
and deliver it to the right place.

Fingered Lace

My mother's new snowsuit
got caught on a fence
that she was not meant to climb over
in much the same way
that Rapunzel's mane
stuck like ivy to the brick of her tower.
My mother's mother saw her
and raced her to the front door;
where, caught,
the other mother
felt her stomach
tie itself into a knot.
The older mother won the race
and put the younger mother in her place.
This is the circuit that I trace –
I, who wasn't made then,
who wasn't even a loop on my mother's finger.
I am still trying to catch them up.

Springtime

In the aftermath, my psychologist tells me to be my own mother.
'Close your eyes and hope for rain,'
I say to myself,

swaddled in the duvet again.
Not the mother I had, but the one I think I need –
(or – has it occurred to her – the one I could have been?)

'Close your eyes,' I say to myself,
trying to aim a spoon of honey at my lips in the dark,
to will the sky to open up,

to be my own pair on the ark.
I cannot sleep. I peer in the mirror,
catching a glimpse of reflected blue sky.

As Big as a House

It's no good telling me to lie back and think –
doing that, I can see my god directly.
It's the roof, and has failed me.

(Either that or I misunderstood what it is that gods do –
forgot, for a moment, about Leda,
and Callisto – Ganymede, too –)

How did you get in here?
Disguised as a bird?
You may have heard that I dream of a house left open for birds to
    fly through.

It doesn't matter that I didn't stay pregnant.
I have been as big as a house,
unlocked, but broken into –

Sextina

See Sextus slip
into Lucretia.
She didn't want to let him but he told
her he'd kill her and wreck her repute too. Do
you see how grittingly, today,
she wills herself away.

Or: In spite of herself Lucretia feels her guard slipping away.
Slip
into me, whispers she. Today
with a sigh she side-steps enmity. See Lucretia
cheating on her husband. The adulteress Lucretia will not do
as she is told.

Or: *I told*
you to go away,
says Lucretia to herself all day. *Do*
promise to avenge me! she says to her family and then *slip*
goes the blade into her belly as – crazy all the while, see – Lucretia
    kills Lucretia
today.

Or: Today
someone told
me that there was no way Lucretia
could get away
with murder. Hell-bound Lucretia is tried posthumously. Slip
into the back of the courtroom to watch. *See what a woman like*
    that can do.

Or: *What was she to do?*
is what I thought, today.
I am sure Lucretia gave Sextus the slip
just like I myself told
you to go away.
I'm like Lucretia.

Or: See Sextus slip into Lucretia.
Do
you think they'll put him away
today?
It depends on how we read her mind. Truth be told,
he's not the one on trial. This wasn't *his* slip.

What are we to make of you, Lucretia?
Today, and today, however the story is told,
away you slip quietly, into the fold.

Admission

At work, a woman talked to me;
her words stuck in my gut like a wet ball of dough.
I let myself go.

It was storming outside.
I thought of the beach.
Mum, on a towel, was baking like a peach.

Her skin looked like orange tulle,
scratchy and forbidding
and beautiful.

I went to whisper in her ear,
but she stopped me
and wrapped her arms around me.

It burned,
where she touched,
and I needed her like the sun.

Little Red Herring

I don't know why they took the prom-night picture like that:
coveralled grandpop squeezed into a corner by the fridge,
mum perched obliquely across his lap.
Long white gloves lapped at her elbows.
Roses swam in his eyes.
In a left-hand window, a bone-coloured moon was on the rise.
There's a herringbone stitch called
jump from one line to the next,
in which the nineteen-nineties succeed the nineteen-sixties,
and a thirty-year patch
of angular open-work
separates the lines with an X.
I was born into that gap
and lapped ceaselessly
at a shoreline
that was not mine and was forbidden to me:
the coast of family.
There can be no comparing of families, no choosing between;
even to fit into one
I would need to have been
as thin as a fish, and neat and mean.

In the Pantry

On the top shelf: onions, beans,
cereals, saltines,
a jarful of millet, tins of sardines.

On the middle shelf: honey, jams in sachets,
popcorn and cocoa for cold days,
crushed tomatoes, three kinds of pasta, lentils.

On the bottom shelf: cigarettes, candles,
wine and liqueurs,
evidence of mice.

Poetry cannot improve upon the beauty of the pantry;
intended as an absence, a catalogue will *suffice*.
It's the middle of the night. I bury my face in my hands and lean
    against the rice.

Floor

My ideal floor can't be found in this house: in this house, unless I
    put thick socks on,
the kitchen carpet, packed with grease,
sticks to my feet.

How's that for a dream house – it's not!
The floor I dream of is somewhere else,
is warm and smells like polish.

I'll pad upon it in slippers,
or nothing at all,
and be home.

(Until then the word itself is almost enough – floor
is the most beautiful word I can think of, except maybe for roof –
I hope I will never have to choose between them.)

Roof

Love's hard to see from above:
it's easy to do,
harder to know if someone's doing it to you.

There's Jesus – for some to believe in –
for me there are rooves, which also need believing in.
A roof isn't quite like a floor.

You don't touch it, though you could.
You could take it apart to see what it is made of, only
then it wouldn't work.

(Loving isn't quite like being loved –
each is everything, and neither is enough –
I hope I won't always have to choose between them.)

Fancywork

Not accidentally, nor by cunning,
do those shapes come;
not painfully, but worked
beneath the fret of talk.

See the women talking there –
pointedly, and debonaire,
in the sunset –
see, below the talk, their hands net and net.

Slowly, the shapes come:
a laced ambush, a netted siege,
a threaded treatise on something unsaid
that was meant.

Their mouths go,
but their hands go faster, meaning something else.
Inside, a dozen antimacassars
rush the peak of every chair.

Fall at French Bay *or* Fall at the Saugeen Reserve

October brings the end of the garbage collection.
Our flags and windsocks grind the breeze like teeth.
Cottages peel from the beach's ice-hard body,
flaps of skin as thin as lace.
Off comes the lake's warm coverlet:
here is the network of frozen cysts.
The neighbour's girl, cupped in a cold dune, panics quietly while
parents pad their cars.
A gloved young man prods the lake, annoyed
and unaware of what he's hunting.

We woke up here all summer, toes first:
bathed in the glow of the bar heater,
dunked ourselves in the water.
Poised to toss, we saw no one behind us
reflected in the horseshoes' iron sheen.
The pines at night sound like wind in my hair,
not like the sound of someone whispering.
I don't remember hearing the garbage truck,
nor noticing the driver.

Where the Beasts Are

One night,
she was full of beasts

(or at least,
the beasts within her reared up).

They weren't the beasts of illness, I think –
these were other, private beasts, that shimmied down

and shook her.
I crept down and took her

sorrows at face value
as she taught me to do,

saying 'no one can ever tell you
what wilds are within you.'

The Fall

I walked into my present
a second too late.
Your arrow missed and hit my brain.
And here I am quite useless, now,
all swollen head and inauspicious heart.

What if I had known?
I could have coursed down
an alternate path: down one of those veins
that skirts my errors
and siphons my secrets.

I say to myself that I would have flown,
that wings were what I wanted
to get to you ahead of time.
This surprise love is vertical,
it has not run along beside me like a river:

the heights to which it threw itself appear only in descent,
like a geyser;
its heights are not made of concrete,
but of water,
without footholds.

I would have needed to catch you before you fell, or before the lift
    cable snapped, or whatever. Now how can I know what you
    were doing up there, just before,
in the height when it was a height unto itself, not unto a fall.
Was I just then on my way up to meet you – couldn't these things
    come to
love as well as death?

I can only write about
what I wish you would have.
I can only say that I don't know
why we write poems after things have happened instead of when
    they are useful,
before, not after, the précis.

Bath

In the bath
the numbers wash off my spine.
This year's nine

disasters burst with the soap bubbles – goodbye!
The letters fall off too:
my name goes down the overflow drain.

I hope it won't come back again,
and then my hopes evaporate:
shapes exhaling, deflating. You're coming up the stairs –

I can hear your ring on the railing –
by the time you get here, I'll be sailing out at sea,
no more than a boat.

Aphorisms for Afternoons

You wouldn't know from the look of me
how hard my heart is beating.

I can't tell which of three things you might feel towards me.
I'm on a game show all the time . . .

I sashay down the corridor.
Three hundred women sashay down the corridor.

A man and a woman might be two sides of a triangle.
A man and a woman might be a Pythagorean set.

Shall I be honest or strategic in this –
(A car alarm goes off across the road.)

Some days, for some reason,
the building groans with malaise.

I could live on reading and writing;
a splendid façade can appear to be a building.

But I know, too, that love requires a boiler room,
and that I require love.

Forgetting the lecture, I notice the doorframes – perfect, severe –
they remind me of ecstasy.

Sometimes the pull of love has scared me,
as gravity would scare a glass perched on the lip of a bench.

Dog

'My mind's like . . . a mushroom,'
the woman says.
'I don't know, but some of it's over there.
I can feel it flowering.'
'What do I think?' the woman also says, or thinks.
She pushes up her sleeves and closes her eyes.
The clock strikes two, quietly,
her pens and the pamphlets she has folded sit perfectly in order,
and she thinks about someone.
She thinks about sending a message to someone,
herself *in absentia*,
a message that gets it right.

A dog travels, down the road, and up the stairs,
bringing with it what it is:
glistening coat, plain health,
silent legs, an easy and silent pace,
up the stairs, and past the photocopier,
and into the office of whom the woman is thinking.
The man turns and there is the dog in the mouth of the cubicle.
The dog has arrived and is breathing at the mouth of the cubicle.
The dog breathes an air of brown fur into the papery blue.
Nothing happens except that man and dog are silent
and the cubicle turns into a sort of mouth
and the woman sits with closed eyes.

In the Hearts of Houses

He turned himself in, that was some time ago, and it's Christmas
    now.
It doesn't matter how warm the house gets, there is always going
    to be
that hole by the furnace. I mean, I don't know whether to think
that because every family has at least one sawed-out hole beneath
    the carpet
I ought to be comforted
or feel that there is no escape from anything.
You don't know
if that hole is there for you too, to hide in, in emergencies,
like in a bad dream when you need 18 doors to lock behind you
    at least;
or whether it is the plug hole
beneath this thing we're keeping together like cooling bathwater
so that if someone just nudges the plug accidentally with their toe
we're all going to go down the drain
where the bad things go.

His Sister

Even now, his sister is not a fan of poetry.
That is exactly how she puts it: 'I am not a fan.'
It says something about her,
the fact that she does not like poetry
even though she likes floral valances and Trisha Romance prints,
or maybe it says something about poetry.
She sticks mostly to thrillers.
In the end we stick to what we know,
not because we wouldn't prefer something else,
but because we wouldn't know it if we saw it.
Her life is metal on the inside, pastels on the outside.
The opposite of this might be a house with nice books in it.
Never would a unicorn figure into it, however you invert it;
the kind of thing a unicorn is will *not* lance into this equation
    from the side.
Her life is a horse to mount and ride.

Boiling Point

No one is going to tell you what they did when they were kids.
Someone might point to the stacks of family photographs
while minding something else, like the peas on the stove.
You could guess a poem, based on that motion,
and try to write something about that
which you could then read something into,
looping the process of poetry right round and through,
like shoelaces do.
Like shoelaces, you will find that you can tie up this story
as many times as you like, and really get the hang of it,
like riding a bike, but you will find that, like shoelaces,
it will always keep coming undone.
Watch not to get tangled in the spokes.
No one is going to go barefoot either; this is Canada, there is snow.

Polar Bear in a Snowstorm
or My Parents' Lounge at Christmas

Bear with me, polar bear; you're the only thing I know is there.
(Reader, it's true – I've left you –
but don't go, mistletoe. I need you to stand under,
even though I might be twenty people passing by,
or only a lingering two.)

A snowstorm covers the hill.
Fire snaps in the fireplace.
My eyes are wide open with tension. My stomach is too full of
      food.
Thank goodness it *looks* good in here; it's times like these
that the lilac-laden wallpaper is just made for papering over.

Bear with me, white thing hidden in the whiteness.
Because I can't see you, I need you there.
The rest of the world, packed with shape and colour, is all too
      present,
and gives too much of itself
without meaning anything by it.

The present world is on fire
with tinsel tones
and the high-toned pink pierce
of Christian women
wanting me for their own.

Bear with me, absent, snow-cool thing.
Stay just there.
I need to imagine
that I can feel you breathing
and your hands in my hair.

Angel

To create evidence
of an angel,

with no mortal footsteps
leading away from or to,

I stood up on the fence-rails
and flopped down into the snow,

holding my arms and legs
wide open.

The ice
stabbed me through.

I became an ice palace,
Shot through with sleet.

I miss her.
She, too, was pierced.

At the hospital,
in a pale disc of light,

our arms lined with cool,
we dared not touch, and formed a balance.

harry
JONES

Beyond Hinuera

Swimming

Swimming, I count each lap
Stroke by stroke, exhale
Number in a rush of breath –
All evens on my back, where
I follow the progress of the moon
Declining into daylight blue.

If this were all there were
To it – physique, number, a blank
Heaven – but it's not.
The mind that perceives, the hand
That pulls, float on depths
That do not light with morning.

Beneath, beyond, the unlit dark
Shadows my progression,
The lengths I aim at, my comfortable
Limit, final number – shadows
My touch to the wall, my climb
Into immediate nakedness.

Three-Finger Exercise

'I think I'll kill myself
When I can't make love.' Thus
You, eighteen, sprawling naked
On a sofa, walking with three fingers
Through the dragging little curls
On a mound above a furrow
Closing heated on my seed. 'Imagine
Being someone's boring wife.
I'd rather take my life.' Below us,
The cars go round Hyde Park. I turn
To you playing in your hair,
Wondering at the rhyme, at a crash
I saw years ago down there.
He wasn't speeding, it wasn't dark,
And he could hardly hold his tears
At a crumpled fender. Most are
Like him at the wheel. They
Can do nothing when they scare.

Freedom

How I love it when you sleep
Without a nightshirt and I wake
To find you naked. It's not
Wanting sex with you – it's more
Some loose idea of the primitive,
A notion of uninhibited self
Being better than covering up,
And there's the feeling too
That body leads somewhere beyond.

It's all pretence, of course –
There is no further knowledge,
No experience to be had beyond
The usual. Every barrier remains.
Body is body still, and ours
Our own. Yet when we move against
Each other, we imagine, or I do,
That there's some transforming advance
From day-to-day realities.

I look around, though, and think
That every such supposed advance
That has been made leads
Nowhere. Your body and mine
Become more common daily.
Ours is a world in which bodily
Obliteration – the finger touch
Shredding limb and limb –
Fixes every fantasy of liberation.

Your body, stretched unawares
On the sheet, has invited murder,
Been slung from ankles, wrists,
Into ditches, ovens, onto stacks
Of countless naked others
By those who know truly that

There is no other barrier to freedom –
Armies, lovers, other willing hands –
Than the purely physical.

One Hour

I was paying a woman
To massage me. I said,
'Let's change – I want to
Do this to you.' 'Alright,
But it's your time
You know,' she said and
Lay where I had been.

Under my hands her skin
Was as fine as planking
Buffed with steel wool,
No blemish to the touch,
And I prepared a boat
For varnish, uniformly smooth
To palms, fingertips.

Then it was the feel of
Polished calfskin, covering
A Book of Common Prayer,
Felt for loss and comfort,
And her lips opened
Like India paper, delicate,
Strange, on a random page.

The Blade

'What parts of my life
Do you think I like?'
He's stabbing the words
With a kitchen knife.

Next he turns on the kid –
'I said shut your face.'
But his wife's in the way –
She's found a pot lid.

These must be the parts
Of his life he means –
The arcs he describes,
Almost like hearts.

Look. Chopping at the air,
Slicing up bits of his life
And cutting off theirs,
Until there's nothing there.

Beachfront

I have come here to die – under
These deep blue skies, the passing,
Pale, flimsy, clouds. I have called
Out, 'What will become
Of me?' Called out – screamed
Inwardly – and never answer back.

I won't ask such a question again.
It's too foolish of a man, too
Idiotic a demand. I would
Rather contemplate the sea, how
It curls and shatters, sweeps
Among the shells.

These, as they litter backwards
With the water, make a sort of
Conversation. They say, 'Nothing
Will become of you, nothing
More than came of us.'

What silly voices people every
Human fantasy. All imagination lies.
This sky, this sea and I form
A firm reality. If there's more,
I never set eyes on it before. It's why
I have come here to die.

Pile-up

I never drive to Auckland, but I see
Some out-of-control kid – number-plate
Spelling something fierce – just make
A corner or avoid a head-on when
Overtaking. Either that or a family –
Children climbing all over the seats –
No one strapped in, going for all
It's worth. It makes it a hell of a journey.

I wonder what they make of me? Just
Another straight-arse in the way? Or perhaps
I'm not even there, don't even figure
In the mind or exist on the road. And
Yet, if you believe what you read,
It's a man like me – everything to live for,
Loaded – who, in an instant, swerves
Directly into an ordinary family car.

Why? What's so bad about succeeding?
Or is it that these others drive without
Reflection? It's true that most of them
Get home – most of all of us, in fact.
And what's left behind? A certain
Peeling off of recklessness and care,
Shavings from the sides, plastic, shreds
Of tyre tread, the glint of can or bottle.

And this loss, this litter, does it count
In the scheme of things? The blood
On the road is hosed into the gravelly
Earth, the gradual leach of humanity –
From its edges, at the centre – all
Is replenished, made good. What words –
Made good. There is belief, in spades.
It hits in a solid fog. Enabling carnage.

Looking at Lucretia

I hope I never come to hear a woman
Pleading for her life, and this before
She's propped against a wall and
Rammed with a car. Or was this
Before or after she was raped, before
Running over her a few times?
I forget. Her hands were tied.

And yet, I've often contemplated
Lucretia, her arms outstretched
To fend off Tarquin's high, waving
Knife. He has one bare knee already
Between hers. I've looked into the eyes
Of both, absorbed in Titian's mastery
Of paint. How are these different?

Both, surely, are cultural artefacts,
One way or another. They each
Complete a search for the transforming,
Lasting moment. Both use
The dreadful panic of a woman
Watching, realising, the inescapable
Man. One made the daily papers.

The other graced the Fitzwilliam
Museum wall, where it helped me see
Beyond it. This piece of news, though –
Where does it screw the mind,
Except into ordinary horror?
It makes me want to frame this woman's
Fear, like Lucretia's, for future gaze.

I have none of Titian's brilliant, loose
Grasp of colour. But nor, I hope,
Do I have the diminishing angle of
The radio report. Here, I heard,

The police had arrested a man. She,
Though, wasn't a woman, but
A sex worker. The pitiful slut.

By way of veracity, I can add that
This took place one night or morning
In Christchurch, New Zealand, in late
December 2005. There's an art gallery
There. Like the Fitzwilliam, I know
Something of what it shows. It has nothing
Of the power of Titian. It wants this.

The Maori Chess Champion

A balding man, grey hair cropped close
To his sunburnt scalp, proclaims
Via his t-shirt, 'Life is a bitch,
Enjoy her'. His wife, under her mask
Of make-up (guessing at the relationship),
Looks weary. When they leave –
This is a hotel breakfast, on the beach
In Bali – their place is taken straightaway
By a young couple. The woman,
Exquisitely shapely, wears a shift
Of cheesecloth over the briefest of bikinis.
I used to smoke, but now I loathe
The pale envelope that drifts from others
Over me. Between mouthfuls, she stands
Her knife and fork vertically on the table.

In Scotland I met a man who told me,
However it came up, that he was the Maori
chess champion. Some years before,
Maybe as many as ten, he'd played
And beaten another visitor who
Claimed to have that title. Rarely
Playing since, not losing,
He kept the continuing honour.
And I knew a girl once, attractive,
Whose mother had told her in seriousness
That she was sitting on a gold-mine.
She meant, I guess, that she
Should aim to travel, not sell out
To first-comers or, as it were, too cheaply.

What is it holds civilisations together?
Tony talks in terms of a nation's
Propaganda. The United States, he says,
Has freedom; Thailand, where he lives,
Respect. But, he adds, people turn

Cheats and liars, and the outcomes
Don't always resemble
The promise of the words. On the way
Back to my rooms, through
The lush, immaculate hotel garden,
I notice I do not recognise the birds.
In Beijing, so someone said who's seen it,
They counterfeit the bags – the branded
Carrier bags – and hawk them on the street.

History

Make no mistake. I am constantly
On the edge of explosion. I have
A wood shredder on the piggery, and I
Take buckets of guts some place
Weekly, where they'd never think
Of looking. It's how I work.

When my kids step out of line,
It's the same. I take a belt to them
Until they're quiet. Then I leave
Them curled up in their pools of stuff.
It gives them time to think.
Believe me, it's how they'll learn.

The demeanour you describe, slow
To anger, patient, steady, is not mine.
It may look that way at times
But never trust it. There's another
Continuance I keep to – violent,
Sudden, glad to use my feet and fists.

Within me, my parents and theirs before
Stay up at night to fight, smother
The young, starve the old, ignore
The way yells carry. This is how
History progresses, pressing those
Calling for love hard against a wall.

A Grey Silk Shirt

'You will forget me,' you said,
'And bring nothing of this to mind,
But I will think of it.'
And so shall I. As I remember
Being a child at a lake, and
Watching the turning breezes make
The surface scatter
In eddies of light, I remember,
Like a revelation,
Your grey silk shirt,
And a string of pearls
At your open neck, and pushing
Into your body, like a boat,
With my foot on the sand, and hearing
A distant stand of trees roar
Like breakers carried
From a further shore, and seeing
The pearls and your shirt and
On my watch the minute hand.

Upskirt

I'll tell you why
I like to reach
Under your skirt.

It's partly your skin,
Astonishingly smooth
To my fingertips.

It's your skin.
So it's you,
In a way, I touch.

And it's not you.
And it's not me.
Flesh does that.

Or maybe it is
Just you. Just me.
I feel that too.

There's a boundary
Between flesh and
Flesh. A limit.

But there's no
Boundary between
Us. I feel that.

And no boundary
Between us and
Something

Beyond us two.

Australia

The most beautiful things on earth
To me – if beautiful means desirable,
And I'm not sure that it does –
Are parts of a woman's body.

I'm transfixed with passion for the flesh
On the inside of female thighs.
I can contemplate it for hours, touching,
Or trying to touch it with my mind.

I have almost as strong a feeling for trees,
To put things in perspective. These
And open country: grassland dotted
With rising trunks and spreading branches.

I look down on land like this, just as
At your limbs, whenever I'm flying into
Melbourne, but with the feeling I could
Live there. To take nothing away from you.

Shining

This is how it was. The blunt stones
On the road shone, the sharp gravel
Glittered. Even the bits of grit
Between the gravel, these shone.

When the dust rose from the road
It coated the wild grass with white –
A different white, unlike the reflecting
White that every blade presented.

The logging trucks threw up most
Of the dust. They shone only in parts.
The forests were plentiful and the logs
Queued at the mill, shining in piles.

Some things shone most. The face
Of a wing mirror, the curve of chrome,
A round hubcap when it was hosed,
The water that streamed from the nozzle.

When I see the place now, I don't
See the same shining. It'll be there
Though, right down in the dust,
In the smallest particles of the road.

Beyond Hinuera

Driving through this still, green
Valley – once a riverbed, but
Lifted clean above the water
In some ancient cataclysm –
I think that many ordinary
Lives are most or best
Remembered, even extended,
Through trees like these.

These massive heads of foliage
Were dug in as saplings once –
A hopeful spade peeling back
Coarse lumps of turf – and
The roots heeled in under
The almost delicately managed
Pressure of a scuffed and muddy
Boot. Someone took this care.

They chose to plant along
The fence lines, or here and there
On the open rise and fall of
The working fields, I suppose
As windbreaks, cover for stock,
But also in the sense or knowledge
That time would make them monumental,
Lend dignity to private lives.

And it has. These full canopies
Stand huge, like nothing so much
As the explosions of earth
Photographed from the trenches
Of France, Belgium, Gallipoli –
Great mounds of farmland flung
Into the air. Did those who planted
These see the plantings there?

Commedia

I saw our vacuum cleaner, the grey
Tellus, had been dragged into the edge
Of the tide. The long, ribbed hose
Looped to the side in an open 'S'
In and out of the brown, gritty sand.

I picked the body of it up
By the handle and felt and heard
The weight and slosh of water
With guilt and disappointment.
I was involved in what had happened.

I carried it to the garden shed and
Left it on the floor, a unique object
On the bare wooden boards.
I decided to bring things from a second shed
Into this one for safe-keeping.

This other had a surprising collection
Of tools – I noticed new screwdrivers
Which I didn't know we owned.
I chose a clutch of wire brushes, one
With brass wire that I use on my suede shoes.

Bolting the door of the first again,
I discovered its hinges all hung free
And how easily it fell open. Just then
My sister leaned over the gate and smiled.
She was young and, behind her, sun.

Cleaning Shoes

You old charmer, wastrel, dreamer, sad man, fraud –
I cleaned your shoes, pairs of black and brown leather
Lace-ups, polished them on the bench under the grape-vine
Trellis, for years. It was my job. What was yours?

It should have been being my father. I stood at the fence
Beside you, waist high, hand in a pocket like yours,
In belted shorts, jacket, tie, even a pocket handkerchief like yours,
For the photograph I have. Boy, was I proud. What a picture.

I tried my hardest, step after step, to make my shoes crunch
Like yours, the time you walked out and along the gravel road,
After that row with my mother. I had to choose. I did. I went
With you, breathless, to the wonderful noise of your walking.

My short, light footsteps made no such sound. I watched
You walk from me once, a last time – leaving me
Behind, pressed under the heavy hand of a stranger –
Along the short, sunny, turning drive. One shoe after another.

The Plum Tree

Two men are at the plum tree, one
Up in the boughs with a chainsaw,
The other feeding the shredder.
It's not ours, it's our neighbours',
But it's what we see, or have done,
Above the trellis, from our bedroom.

It's large. It overhangs their washing line,
Dominates that stretch of lawn, fills
An area of sky in our usual view.
It hosts a pair of rosellas, among
Other occasional birds. It has nothing
To do with us, aside from seeing it.

By rights, they can fell the whole
Thing if that's what they wish.
We felled a big old plum tree here,
And I grew up with many fruit trees –
My parents had them, and they've gone.
As each branch falls, it alters the light.

Curtains

We have no curtains this end
Of the house. We don't bother
With them and haven't done
Since renovating. We didn't
Re-hang the old ones. I threw them
Onto the skip of builders' rubbish –
And saw the light green folds of fabric
Disappear over a couple of days
Under bricks, plasterboard,
Timber, sweepings, lengths of pipe.

One day we took the rails down,
Bending them backwards –
Not easy, one of the edges cut me –
Unscrewed the fittings, and
The decorators painted and papered
Over every hole and trace.

Without curtains, the windows,
The French doors, are hard
Edged. They sit in a symmetrical
Architecture of aluminium.
A blank, rigid pattern
Of horizontals and uprights
Frames the sheets of glass.
You could say they lack a little
Softness, maybe humanity.

There's no shortage of curtains.
Most houses have them. They appear
In books, magazines, on television,
In shops, in thoughts, calculations,
Conversations, wishes, gestures,
Quarrels, silences, invoices,
Promises, threats, parcels – in more
Things than are worth listing.

Because we have no curtains,
We see the dark when it comes
In the evening, shutting
The garden in impenetrable black.
It's there at the glass until –
and when – we leave for bed, turning
Off the lights in the kitchen,
The breakfast room, the drawing room.
It fills the house behind us.

But, until we head off, tired,
We don't merely see the dark. We see
Ourselves, reading, talking, making
Love, listening to music, watching
The news, drinking tea, coffee, glasses
Of wine – at weekends maybe a brandy
Or port – sitting or in movement,
Features imperfectly defined, lit
By the glow of standard lamps,
The picture light over the landscape,
Photographs on the tray tables,
Other pictures, sofas, the big
Table, scattered books, toys, papers.

We see this – more – with each other,
Maybe one or both of the cats,
A metre of two of the verandah,
And, occasionally, a lighted window –
If that's what it's called –
Visible through the robinias
In one of our neighbours' houses.
It could be an upstairs kitchen.
It discloses nothing of their lives.

We have looked at curtain fabric,
Discussed cedar blinds, roman blinds,
Various rails, pleats and folds,
A number of fabric options. We
Had someone round to measure

Every window in the house.
Our names, the dimensions, will remain
In the system for a while, even
Though we mayn't use them. In time,
Doubtless, they'll be deleted.

It's more than possible, though,
That some day we'll hang curtains,
And draw them over the windows,
The French doors, at night, closing
Them on the outside world.
It's perfectly possible – after all,
We've made no decision
Never to have curtains again.

True, too, we made no decision
In favour of the dark, no choice
To see these black areas of glass,
With ourselves, other reflections. These
Have happened as no consequence
Or act of will, no discrimination
In their favour or notions of taste.

If we choose to go with curtains
There will be a colour or colours,
Shapes, structures, a texture,
Tones, perhaps a pattern,
That I cannot imagine – where
There is just glass, where at night
We see ourselves and our surrounds,
The two of us, others sometimes,
Doing whatever we're doing
As usual this end of the house.

Out of the Dark

Always tomorrow, and after that
The next day – and the dawn comes
Up a blank behind the pine trees,
And patches them into the ridgeline,
Adds in the scrub, the yellow of gorse,
The slope of the gully, and finishes.

The same high climb of farmland
Flames at its limit just before dark,
And then it is night, dissolving
The pines on the ridge, uprooting
The gorse, pitching all into black.
I read by a light, sink under covers.

And sleeping is motion. A rustling
Of the undergrowth, a fling out
On the air, a digging for sustenance,
A prowl at the fence line – where
Morning discloses a still, spread-eagled
Hedgehog afloat in the horse trough.

Little creature. I spade it out of the water
In a splash of sunlight, in ripples
Repeating those of its dying, when
Drive or adventure brought it this end.
I dig a grave in the shade. The soil is dark.
I too search for answers at night.

On the Canterbury Plains

How still this expanse of country lies –
The gesture of the trees forgotten
Where they stand, the brown
Indifference of distant hills fixed
In a final shrug, like sleepers rolled
Into immobile, thoughtless comfort.

To look on this, you'd think creation
Had come to an end, the world complete,
The point made, the day's objectives
Met, and all will stay as it is – vague
Birds choosing this post top or
That, the grass doing its duty to the breeze.

The few more movements – the drift
Of seeds, an erratic butterfly, a ripple through
Leaves – flicker in the eye, the mind,
Complete their containment, lock
Them fast in the solid spread of farmland,
In the warm, dozing afternoon of fields.

Such stillness. And not silent, but alive
With crickets, fragments of birdsong,
Distant noise. All this combined,
And nothing to add, this is a lifetime's
World. The plains pause in the sunlight,
Blinking, arms outstretched, engine humming.

After the Flood

When we walked this way last
It was different. The iron bridge
Was as far as we could go.
Along this muddy path we waded,
The trees rooted in pools of water.
It was the last of the snow.

And it was cold. We stood awhile
Against these rails, the river
Twisting fast beneath our feet. Now
There's nothing of it. Far down it curls,
Silent, dark right to the edge,
Bearing a shifting weight of clouds.

It was a flooding race and rip
Right through this further field.
Beneath us is some hidden moving,
And you and I reflected with the sky
Are all that can be seen of it. Ahead
The grass is soft and shines.